THE *One* THING

100 Widows Share Lessons on Love, Loss, and Life

Kerry Phillips

Dedicated to Cianna

*"In the same way I will not cause pain without
allowing something new to be born,"
says the Lord*

To The Widow Beginning Her Grief Journey,

I once stood right where you are - unsure if I was capable of accepting the reality of my situation. Uncertain if the weight of being a young widow would crush me. There is a numbness, a disconnect between our brain and reality. This was not supposed to be our life.

The cancer diagnosis...the accident...the drugs...the heart attack...the suicide...none of these were present in the talks of our anniversaries...our travels...our children...our retirement...our happily ever after.

I won't tell you the road ahead will be easy. I won't tell you that you'll come out of it the person you were before your loss. But, I will tell you that it's going to be okay. This doesn't mean that you'll go back to life as you knew it though. That old you, that version of you that existed before the death, she is no more. You'll be left with pieces of her...parts you must somehow include in the framework of your current circumstances. I encourage you to take the very best of who you were (the wife who juggled a career and children while taking care of her spouse and the one who stood by his side as he took his last breath) and bring her with you as you ultimately become the fierce, independent, solo-parenting warrior that grief will eventually mold you into.

Be kind and patient with yourself. You determine your path to healing. You don't owe anyone an explanation for how you choose to grieve. Be safe and protect your children at all costs. Find a support system or a close girlfriend who you trust to be open and honest with you, regardless of how much the truth hurts. There are times we fall so far down into the black hole of despair that we need someone to let us know when we're self-sabotaging and behaving in a manner that is counter-productive to our healing.

Respect your grief. You can't out-run, out-drink, out-sex or out-medicate it. If it becomes too heavy a burden, seek out professional help, at the very least an online support group. There is no shame in realizing you're unable to go it alone. It takes a brave person to do a complete inventory of herself and know when she's not equipped to handle the depression and anxiety.

There is no one size fits all. Your "Year Two" doesn't have to be your worst year as it is for so many widows. Use the advice from others and grief books as a guideline. Year markers are not set in stone and neither are the stages of grief. Acknowledge the feelings and grief waves as they come. Look ahead with positivity but live in the moment. If you're overwhelmed by what's to come, focus on getting through the next hour, the next day. Celebrate your victories. Let them serve as motivation to know that you can and will get through this pain.

The goal of "The One Thing" is to share insights and words of wisdom from those who are farther along in their grief...the one lesson they've learned in their respective chapters.

Though no two widows grieve the same, it is my wish that their "one thing" guides you through the early stages of widowhood and beyond. I hope you'll also learn that while there is no "right" or "wrong" way to grieve the loss of a spouse, there can be "healthy" and "unhealthy" ways. Do what feels right to your spirit and soul. Everything you need to get to a place of healing is within you, even the ability to know when a professional therapist is needed.

Please return to this book often, as it explores topics that may not be applicable to this stage of your grief but can be relatable weeks, months or even years from now.

Most importantly, as you move through your healing process, remember to reach back and help the next wave of young widows. Share your lessons, your advice, your coping mechanisms...your "ONE THING".

TABLE OF CONTENTS

GRIEF

"Give yourself time to heal.
Grieving is not an overnight
process. It will hurt every
day for a long time. But,
one day you'll wake up and
realize it no longer
hurts every day."

You have to let grief in. I fought it for a year by dating too early and going on trips I can't even remember. Once my relationship ended, grief appeared and it was not taking no for an answer. I spent Year 2 on my knees or balled up on the bedroom floor. I eventually joined a widowed support group and met local girlfriends. It's been great being able to reach out to someone when I'm in the pit of grief.

Cyra, Widowed August 2014

"I talk about my husband all the time. I'm at a place in my grief where I can laugh about and at him. He'd want that. I'm doing what I think he would have wanted."

To this day, I don't think I've taken the time to fully grieve. I was my husband's caregiver for two years prior to his death and perhaps some grieving was done during that time. I took two months off from work after he died but I was in a daze. I then threw myself into a new job which was a major distraction. Meditation became a way for me to handle my grief and I credit it with saving my life. It forced me to turn off my brain and not think of anything. It was through meditation that I was able to finally give myself permission to let go of much of my pain and sadness.

Margaret, Widowed February 2015

DENIAL.

I've learned that I own my grief and I own my healing. I went to Las Vegas with two girlfriends nine months after my husband's death. It was there that I realized my life had to go on. He would have wanted that for me. When you lose a spouse, the best way to honor him is to live the best life you can. My motto is now, 'Life begins at the end of your comfort zone' and have tried to step outside the box with activities such as going to Burning Man, an annual gathering in Black Rock City. My goal is to lead a life that embodies my favorite hashtags:

#LearningToLiveAgain,
#LearningToLoveAgain, and
#MakingMoments.

Sharon, Widowed July 2015

"Reaching out to someone who gets it can be the lifeline needed to keep going."

People tend not to understand your grief when they don't think you're grieving the way you should. A close relative, for example, has been widowed for 12 years and doesn't seem to get why I'm still so sad about my husband's death. Grief is an individual process. Everyone has to grieve in his or her own way and it's different and unique for each widow.

Cheryl, Widowed August 2014

After my husband died, I remember standing in my bathroom, opening the medicine cabinet and seeing a bottle of OxyContin, left over from having my thyroid removed because of cancer. I didn't want to live through the pain I was in. It then hit me that despite the hurt, I couldn't leave my children orphaned. Instead, I turned to yoga. It was the one place I could find peace. For the first year, I cried through every yoga pose but it was a great release. The poses were painful...like grief...but my body kept pushing through. I eventually got my yoga certification and now teach others who are dealing with a loss. Grief is a feeling and it cannot kill you. Your mind will tell you that you can't get through the pain but it's all about choice.

Jill, Widowed June 2013

"Crying is not a sign of weakness or that you don't want to move forward. It's your body cleansing you. Cry it out."

"When it comes to grief, you have to do what feels right for you."

ANGER.

In the past, I was judgmental and would wonder why a person was doing XYZ while grieving. Now that I've experienced the loss of my husband, I've learned that everyone's grief is different. Grief comes in waves and you just have to go with it. You have to allow it to take you wherever it leads. I found the longer I waited to work through my grief, the harder it was. You truly do not start healing until you do the work.

Pamela, Widowed February 2013

BARGAINING.

"You will always be broken but don't forget to live while grieving."

Kerry Phillips

Grief is ongoing. Sometimes you'll find it appears in a memory while other times, it's right in your face. My two children needed me so I had to push through my grief. As a widow, you have to take things one day at a time. Do the one thing that needs your immediate attention. Some days it's your children and other days it's you who needs the extra care. Focus on that one thing; everything else can wait. If you try to handle it all, you'll end up overwhelmed or losing your mind.

Regina, Widowed August 2015

There's an unpredictability with grief. At times, I think I'm doing great while other times I'm uncontrollably sad. I'm not typically a crier but I found myself crying in public, especially the first two weeks after my husband died. I reached out to a counselor who told me I'd probably cry for the rest of my life and it was okay to let the tears flow through me. She was so right. You often feel so much better after a good cry.

Karina, Widowed March 2015

"When you lose a spouse, you realize you have no control over your life. That can throw your mind for a loop."

"I would force myself to smile 25 times day so it would become a habit. If I smiled, others would feel comfortable. If they felt comfortable, they'd leave me alone. It was exhausting to fake it."

DEPRESSION.

Grief can be so overwhelming. I think it's important for widows to find a support group. Young widows, especially, have different needs than those of a widow in her 70's and 80's. After attending a Hospice support group, I realized the vast differences between young and old widows. For example, while their focus was on their physical ability to do household chores such as pulling trash cans to the curb, my priority was helping my 16-year-old son grieve the loss of his father. I recommend young widows find others who can identify with their issues and share in their grief process.

Kristie, Widowed April 2015

"Sometimes the grief cycle is expected...like birthdays and anniversaries. Sometimes, it's unexpected and creeps up on you while doing mundane activities such as picking out paint."

"Find the resilience to know that while you had a sad/bad day, tomorrow may be better or things will be okay by the end of the week."

"I wish I'd found a support group earlier in my grieving process. Finding so many others going through the same range of emotions was such a relief."

Grief never ends; it just evolves. Sometimes, grief is smiling from a memory and other times, it's a gut punch. You really just have to breathe through every moment because it's hard to process so many emotions at once. Just go with the ebbs and flows of grief and, like a rip current, don't fight it when it happens. Yes, you'll go under but if you let it flow over you, you'll get to a place where you don't end up on the floor - the place where you were a month ago.

Sarita, Widowed May 2015

ACCEPTANCE.

CHILDREN

"Children bring you up from the depth of despair on the days when all you really want to do is lie there."

LOVE.

It's been a challenge preserving my husband's memory for our daughter who was only 5 months old when he died. She's starting to ask about him but doesn't quite grasp the concept of death. I've encouraged one of my stepchildren who was really struggling with his grief to talk to her about their father, which is helping him process his pain in a constructive way. He tells her all the wonderful things he did with my husband and how awesome of a father he was. It's important for them to know that we're still a family and we have to stay connected, despite our loss.

Kala, Widowed May 2014

"The only people I owe anything to are my children."

"I still strive everyday to get parenting right."

All three of my boys had their own unique way of dealing with their father's death. My oldest son took it the hardest and had a brief but drastic downward spiral. My middle child is still angry and blames his father for committing suicide, and my youngest son just 'rolled with the punches' and jumped back into the normalcy of life.

There is no set way for adults to deal with grief and children are no different.

Carole, Widowed April 2014

When your spouse dies and you're trying to restart your life, there are so many transitions, both big and small. Each of these ultimately affects children. It's been important for me to provide stability. They need to know now, more than ever, that certain aspects of their lives will remain the same.

While I do strive for consistency, I teach my children that inevitably some people will come into and leave our lives. You have to teach both sides of the coin. That's key for mental survival.

Tryphenna, Widowed March 2012

"We talk about their father often
so he's still a part of their life.
We work to keep his memory alive."

Coming to terms with the parent I thought I would be with my husband and the parent I am post-loss has been difficult. The truth is, I had to let go of the high expectations I had for myself. I had to accept the fact that his death changed me.

I'm so much more gentle and forgiving, especially with my children. On the days I get really frustrated, I remind myself that in the grand scheme of life, whatever they did wasn't that serious. The only thing that truly matters is that my children know they are loved.

Becky, Widowed July 2015

STABILITY.

"If it weren't for my boys, I would have stayed in bed for at least six months. I knew I had kids to raise so I had to pick myself up and keep going."

My daughter was a month shy of two years old when her dad died. I've made it my goal to make sure she has positive male role models in her life. It's important that she sees how a good man treats a woman.

Julie, Widowed June 2013

When I initially lost my husband, I was afraid to show my emotions because I thought in doing so, I was protecting my children. Eventually, I had to let them realize it was okay to cry and be sad. They needed to know that we were going to get through the loss and be okay. Our grief was a bit different because I lost my husband to suicide. The children had very complicated grief and it was difficult getting beyond 'I wasn't enough' to truly get to a place where they could understand mental illness. Kids model your behavior and getting us into therapy as a family has been a huge part of our healing.

Allison, Widowed September 2012

"We can't live our lives in constant grief. This isn't how life is supposed to be for our children."

CONSISTENCY.

"Too often we try to hide our grief from our kids. Don't."

I didn't realize how difficult it would be being an only parent. When you're divorced, you know you'll have days when you can accomplish the many things you have to tackle - without the children. As a widow, there is no other parent. I know I'm not always my children's favorite person but I pray that when they are 25, 30 years old, they'll look back and see that I really tried and appreciate all I've done for them.

Alicia, Widowed June 2015

Children are very resilient and they take their cues from us. When I had to sit my children down to tell them their father wasn't coming home, my son ran through the house screaming and bawling his eyes out. I was 'ugly girl' crying too, having to see my son so hurt and distraught.

My father, who was there for moral support, calmly said to my son, 'We need to gather some special things because we're going to see your daddy. We're going to get a box, fill it with all your favorite memories, and we'll share it with him'.

My son immediately stopped crying and went to look for things to put in the box. That was my 'aha' moment: my son had followed my dad's example.

I've learned children need to know that everything is going to be okay. We can be sad but we can't stay there indefinitely. Every minute we remain in sadness means we aren't living or experiencing life.

Daphne, Widowed September 2012

PATIENCE.

My husband and I had six children between us. When he passed, I felt it was important for all of them to continue having a relationship. It's been challenging because the youngest was 7 years old and the oldest was 25. But, I still keep family traditions in place and make sure there is ongoing communication between them.

Tina, Widowed January 2015

"Widowhood is harder when our kids are younger because they need more care and widowhood is harder when our kids are older because they understand more."

"My children have already been through a lot so I need people in my life who will show up for them and keep their promises."

"At times it can feel as though we need an act of Congress to be able to have some alone time."

My son was 2.5 years old and I was 22 weeks pregnant when my husband died. I immediately started therapy because I needed to get back to at least 50 percent in order to be ready when she was born. I've had to be everything for my children and though I fail 100 percent of the time, I keep trying. I recently told my mother that I'm terrified of screwing them up. She laughed and said, 'You will. But you'll be there to pick them up!'.

Catherine, Widowed October 2011

IN-LAWS

"Grief can bring
families together or
pull them apart. It all
depends on how that
grief is handled."

I lost my mother at 22 years old. When I got married, I truly embraced my husband's family and thought they felt the same about me. I expected there may be some strain to the relationship the first year after I lost my husband but never imagined there would be tension five years later. I know they are still hurting and I realize the pain will never be gone, but I didn't do anything wrong for them to turn against me. I will always love them. It's also important for me to be cordial for my children's sake. They need to know their father's side of the family.

Kim, Widowed January 2013

UNDERSTANDING.

"I had to establish boundaries and let my in-laws know that I AM the parent and I alone determine my children's future."

"I'm not the only person who lost. My in-laws lost their son - their baby..."

"The greatest gift I was given by my husband is his family."

I come from a family of alcoholics so I gravitated towards my husband's family. I met him when I was 16 years old and his family became my family, much more than my own. After my husband's death, I realized the 20+ years I'd spent building a relationship with them amounted to nothing. I understand that they lost their son/brother so I gave them the space they needed to grieve. They didn't do the same for me. I was accused of always playing the 'widow card' when the truth was, I didn't know how to do life without my husband. I eventually moved to another state to be closer to my cousin who had been one of the few family members with whom I had a relationship. I needed to remove the negativity and toxicity of my in-laws from my life. I won't allow them to hurt me anymore.

Katherine, Widowed July 2014

The greatest gift I was given by my husband is his family. If it weren't for them, I don't know where I'd be. My father-in-law in particular has been my rock. I can vividly recall the family gathering in the hospital room to say our final goodbyes and my father-in-law saying, 'Don't worry, son. We'll always take care of Robin'. He's kept those words until this very day and reassures me our relationship won't end simply because my husband died. It feels good to know his family - which became my family - will always be there for me.

Looking back, there were times during my 'widow fog' that I can see that I took advantage of their love - being needy... seeing how many buttons I could push. They lovingly told me to stop and continued to be there for me through my pain.

When I started dating, I hid it from my in-laws. It wasn't because I thought I wouldn't have their support, I just didn't want to hurt them. When I finally admitted it, they told me they wanted me to find happiness again.

My in-laws have given me so much - love wise - that I could never begin to repay them. They love me unconditionally and have never asked for anything in return. I will always cherish them.

Robin, Widowed November 2012

Having never lost a child, it's hard for me to fully appreciate my in-laws' grief. Over the years, I've come to realize that they are who they are; I won't try to change them. I've changed though. I'm a different person now than when I lost my husband. While I think it's important for my in-laws to be a part of my child's life, I won't work any harder than they do to maintain that relationship.

Heather, Widowed April 2015

SUPPORT.

My husband's siblings seem to think that because my husband died, I no longer exist. I struggled with this for a long time but eventually realized it's not about me. I know they are grieving yet it's been really hard seeing my relationship with them deteriorate. If we hadn't been close prior to my husband's death, then I'd totally get their attitude towards me now. Thankfully, one of my brothers-in-law (the one who practically raised my husband) and I are still close. That helps me feel connected to my husband's family on some level.

Judy, Widowed September 2011

"Although my children miss being able to spend unrestricted time with their grandparents, it's just not worth the ugliness that comes after."

At times, I feel my in-laws call to invite my children to family events as a way to appease their own guilt...to be able to say they did extend an invitation. My very wise cousin gave me great advice which helped me put things into perspective: 'You don't know their grief. You don't know where they are in their pain/sorrow'. She was right; I have to be the bigger person. I make every effort to get my kids to family gatherings, even if my in-laws call the day of the event. While I don't think there is a grandparent/grandchild bond per se, my children are always happy to see their extended family.

Beth, Widowed March 2012

SUPPORT.

"Any problems you have with your in-laws will be ten times worse after a spouse's death. Your 'buffer' is gone - the person who served as the mediator."

Grief can bring families together or pull them apart. It all depends on how that grief is handled. My husband was re-diagnosed on his mother's birthday. I'm not sure if that's what flipped a switch in my relationship with her but everything changed. I know she's grieving...it must be hard to lose a child. It's too bad that we no longer speak because I have a great relationship with the rest of his family.

Amelia, Widowed April 2015

After my husband died, my in-laws were able to spend as much time as they wanted with my children. There were no rules or boundaries which eventually created havoc. When they found out I was dating via the kids, they didn't handle the news well. It really damaged our relationship. Looking back, I wish I would have told my in-laws about my dating on my own terms.

Allison, Widowed December 2014

"Sometimes in-laws need to blame someone for their loss. Unfortunately, most times, it's the surviving spouse."

My therapist suggested I write a letter to my son, explaining the absence of his father's side of the family. It was very therapeutic being able to express my feelings as they were in that moment—with rich and raw emotions. Time has a way of massaging our memories and feelings and it would be difficult explaining the dynamics of the relationship without the context of that period of time.

You assume that in your loss, the people closest to you will be the ones to step up with support, but support tends to come from the most unexpected of places. Was I shocked about my in-laws? No. Disappointed? Yes. I used to have unresolved angst (wondering what I could have done differently) but I had to let it go.

I do feel sorry that they miss out on seeing their son/ brother through my child. He is so much like his father - his mannerism, personality, sense of humor. The him that he is in the world is a small version of his dad.

Taya, Widowed June 2012

COMMUNICATION.

"I had to explain to my mother-in-law that parenting while grieving was the equivalent of standing in the middle of the ocean with both arms up...a child in each hand. I'm struggling to keep my kids above water while fighting to not go under myself. I don't have another hand to hold you up. I cannot be your lifeline."

RESPECT.

"We've established neutral ground - weddings, funerals, etc., - where we agree that we will be cordial."

"I needed to remove the negativity and toxicity of my in-laws from my life."

After my husband died, I felt pressured to keep my in-laws in my child's life - despite their negativity. I often wondered if I was a 'bad person' for wanting to limit their interactions. I wish I'd trusted my gut more because I soon realized it wasn't healthy to put up with dysfunction or abuse. It was not good for me or my child. I had to give myself permission to know what was best for us.

Carrie, Widowed March 2012

FAMILY & FRIENDS

"You have to remind yourself that people aren't ignoring you. Your spouse's death just isn't front and center for them. They don't understand what it's like to lose a spouse so try not to be angry."

My friends were already like family but they became even more so after the loss of my husband. They literally held me up when I thought I couldn't go on. My husband died a week before my daughter's graduation and a neighbor said, 'Don't worry about her. I'll take her to any and all graduation activities she wishes to participate in'. Another friend kept my keys for six weeks and moved my car to comply with city's alt-parking regulations. The support I received from friends and family has made me a more sympathetic and empathetic person. I've also learned the importance of telling others what I really need from them instead of the standard, 'No, I'm fine', response which so many of us tend to give because we don't want to be viewed as a burden.

Arnita, Widowed May 2011

I've lost friends and people I thought were close. No one really wants to talk about my husband anymore. It's almost like out of sight, out of mind. Some friends seem to have a difficult time dealing with the loss while others think I should be 'over' my grief by now. I know they aren't all being malicious but it's hurtful not being able to talk about my husband, even with those who knew him. My brain knows friends may be having a hard time with his death but my heart doesn't get why they can't understand what I'm going through.

Trish, Widowed October 2015

"As you develop a sense of self, tell your friends and family what you need from them."

I try to understand and accept that my husband's death isn't just a loss for me. It is a loss for family and friends too. However, it's still hard losing a lot of friends and family in the process. I was not grieving enough for some. The truth is though, they don't know what happens behind closed doors. I can't fall apart in front of my children; they hate when I cry. I've come to understand that no one has to approve of or agree with my grief. It's part of who I've become post-loss.

Melissa, Widowed April 2015

"My friends thought I was doing 'okay' because they didn't see me crying. But, they aren't there when I'm falling apart in the bathroom."

SUPPORT.

My relationship with my family was definitely strengthened by the death of my husband. Within five hours of his passing, relatives were buying plane tickets and making travel arrangements to be with me. They continue to call and check on me, including on my wedding anniversary. Unfortunately, I can't say the same for all my friends. Those who I thought would run actually stayed and have been there for the past three years. The friends I believed would be supportive are the ones who ran. I've heard some are uncomfortable with my grief while others are afraid to say my husband's name because I will cry. Do they think I've forgotten him? His not being here is a constant reminder of my loss. I would encourage new widows to be careful of what they say to friends. You won't believe how quickly your words can be misunderstood and possibly turned against you.

April, Widowed October 2014

"It's important to assess the relationships we had with friends and family before the death of our spouses. If we only spoke to the person once a year for the holidays, it's unrealistic to expect them to turn into someone else and be there for us the way we need them to be."

Because both my immediate and extended family have experience dealing with death (both young and old), there's been a greater understanding of my loss. Plus, my grandmother - the matriarch of the family - was widowed. She imparted a wealth of information that has helped me navigate my own journey. She cautioned me against telling my son, who was only five months old when his father died, that he's now the man of the house. She did and it caused a rippling effect on the family. At times, I find loved ones expect my life to mirror hers (she went on to earn a Ph.D., helped her children's nanny purchase a home and more) but I have to remind them that although we did lose a spouse at the same age, every widow is different and has a unique story.

Elizabeth, Widowed November 2011

"I remind family and friends that if this isn't the ship they want to get on with me, then jump off. It's where I'm heading and I control the destination."

FRIENDSHIP.

"Some people would rather do nothing than do the wrong thing."

There was an initial shift in my relationship with friends. I think there was a fear factor. They believed I was too sad to enjoy life or hang out. I reminded them that although my husband is dead, I'm still alive. Thankfully, he had encouraged me to spend time with friends and family even as his own health deteriorated. He wanted to prepare me for a future without him. I can recall going to the movies soon after his death. It was my first reminder that I had to live my life. I now know it's okay that every moment of my life doesn't have to be spent in tears. I can be happy.

Victoria, Widowed September 2015

"Don't try to do everything on your own. Your head is not clear, especially in those early days following the death of a spouse."

I was the one who made a change to the dynamics of my relationship with family and friends. They were trying to be there for me but I pulled away. I didn't want to be around people. There were too many memories of happier times associated with them. Even though it's been almost three years since my husband's death, I'm still kind of withdrawn. While I don't think my approach hindered my own healing, it may have had a negative impact on my children. I wasn't there for them as much as I could have been.

Andrea, Widowed February 2015

You truly find out who your friends are when you lose a spouse. I've been surprised by longtime friends who dropped off as well as by the peripheral acquaintances who showed up for me. It's really hard to lose those relationships, especially when we're already hurting. I felt so isolated. It seemed no one knew what to say to me so they said nothing. The whole experience has helped me put things in perspective. I've learned to go towards the people in my life instead of stepping back and letting them do the work.

Melissa, Widowed March 2015

"Friends and family shouldn't have to experience the loss of a spouse or partner in order to understand our struggles."

GENUINE.

My relationships with my close friends have remained unchanged. They've been amazing at remembering the anniversary of my husband's death, our wedding date, and my birthday. They've even made it a point to ask what my plans are for milestone dates. My husband and I had a wonderful network of friends. After his passing, I continued to be included. It's a great social situation with friends' husbands becoming like older brothers I never had. The only 'issues' I've dealt with have been with friends who want me to express myself more and share my feelings. I believe it's their support and prayers that have helped me survive.

Alissa, Widowed May 2013

LOYAL.

It's pretty sad that I've lost so many friends since my husband died. Many of the couples we hung out with have also distanced themselves. Even within my own family, there have been negative changes. Nowadays when I'm invited out, it's almost certainly followed by, '..but if you don't want to come, I understand'. They don't even let me make my own decision to attend or not. It feels at times that I'm a reminder that bad things can happen to people so everyone keeps their distance. I'm learning not to take it personally though. Instead, I'm focusing on things that bring me happiness.

Julie, Widowed January 2015

JUDGMENT

"Don't let anyone's judgment determine your actions. Even if you aren't sure how to handle a situation, let it brew until you figure out what's best for you."

ASSUMPTIONS

"People see my smile and assume
I'm 'over' my husband. The people
closest to me know better though.
A dear friend once said,
'Your smile is there but it's so
hollow'. There is so much
truth to that statement."

INNUENDOES.

Most of the judgment I've received has come from people I thought were friends. Married friends, for example, no longer wanted anything to do with me. They assumed since I lost my husband that I would be after their men. People talked about everything I did - from finances to raising my children. I had to block out the noise and do what was best for me and my family.

Christine, Widowed January 2011

I felt I was constantly being judged by others. Everyone seemed to be watching my every move and questioning my decisions. It turned out I was the one doing the judging - I was judging myself. As widows, we're told that others will judge us and so we have a preconceived notion that friends, family, and even strangers will have something to say about the way we live our lives. I can recall going to friends and saying, 'I don't want you to judge me for this decision but...' and to my surprise, the response continued to be, 'We're so proud of you! We're not judging you at all. You should be so proud of how far you've come'. The reality was that I'd been much harder on myself than anyone else had. Coming to terms with that has been part of the baby steps needed to help me grow.

Caroline, Widowed May 2015

I live in a small town and every time I leave the house, people look at me as though I have three heads. I was recently at a cross-country event for my daughter where a group of women formed a circle and turned their backs to me. I'm not sure if I'm being treated like this because I'm not originally from here, the nature of my spouse's death (suicide), or the fact that I've remarried. It may be a combination of all of those things. Through lots of therapy and self-care, I've learned the judgment is really about the other person and not about me. I'm much more at peace now.

Michelle, Widowed March 2014

"When I receive unsolicited advice, I always say, 'I didn't send you a ballot to vote so you don't get to have an input in my life'."

I felt the most judgment from my church. My husband and I met in the Marine Corps and were very involved in church. After he died, I took a step back. I began working with a veterans organization and met the most incredible group of people who belonged to a motorcycle club. I was sitting with a few members in a dive bar and remember thinking that I'd never felt so accepted. When I eventually returned to church, a congregant asked, 'Oh...you're back hanging with us?' I wanted to tell her to just shut up. Where was she when I'd taken a break from church? How many times did she call to check on me? How many times did she meet up with other members and not extend an invitation? How often did I walk to my car alone after teaching her child in Sunday school? As widows, we have so many losses. I wish she would have offered to pray for me instead of judge me.

Carol, Widowed January 2009

"I find there is a sense of fakeness from people. On social media, everyone wants to comment how they'll be there for you but in the real world, no one shows up."

I think today's widows are judged more harshly because of social media. Our lives are displayed through photos and statuses and people feel they have the right to comment or judge us. I used to hesitate to post photos on Facebook because if you're 'too happy' people think you're 'over' it. Now, I just don't give a damn. I don't care what anyone has to say. I live the hell of having lost a husband every day but I still have to make the most of the life I have left.

Nancyann, Widowed February 2015

"We judge ourselves, especially if there are children involved. We wonder if we're a good enough parent, if we can be more patient, etc., and we often try to compensate for their not having the other parent."

EXPECTATIONS.

About a week after my mother-in-law passed away, my father-in-law mentioned setting up a dating profile. Honestly, I quietly judged him. Three years later, I lost my husband and about 2-3 months into my own widowed journey, I began secretly dating. You truly have no idea what widowhood is like until you've been through it. I had no right to judge Dad. He has not judged me and even invited my new boyfriend to join us for family pictures. He's taught me that it's best to offer support without judgment. It's not our place to judge...just our place to love.

Candalyn, Widowed November 2014

The judgment I've received from others has caused me to lose a bit of faith in people. Very soon after the death of my husband, I had sex with a married friend. We were both grieving my husband's death and bonded over our shared pain. It wasn't the best decision I've made. When something like that happens, it really throws off your moral compass. I confided in what I thought was a close friend and she immediately cut me and my daughter out of her life. She's a very religious person and for her, things were very black or white. It was a harsh lesson to learn and made me re-evaluate the people I could trust.

Rosie, Widowed December 2014

CRITICISM.

It seems to be a trigger for people when you're a young widow. They wonder how'd they'd handle all the situations we face daily and that is projected onto us. When I'm feeling judged, I try to be objective and think about what it is that I'm doing to get that reaction from them. I know now that it's not about me; it's about them. I have to live my truth and not judge them in return.

Gema, Widowed June 2015

GOSSIP.

I've found that it's the people who know you post-loss that you can actually confide in. They seem to be removed from the death so they tend to offer the most unbiased perspective. I lost my dad when I was 9 years old and assumed my mother would be empathetic to my pain. She pushed for me to go to therapy but it wasn't what I wanted. I know she genuinely wanted to help. However, if I don't feel my grief is understood, it's that much harder to make a true connection.

Julie, Widowed May 2015

"Forty-five days after my husband died, I was told to 'come back to the land of the living because he wasn't coming back'. But yet when I live and embrace life, I'm 'over' his death. The judgment we get is so weird."

"How dare someone who goes home and gets in bed with their spouse tell me I am playing the 'widow card'."

"It's hard for people to make decisions about your life when they aren't in your shoes."

There has been such judgment from my family and close friends especially as it pertains to my home. After my husband died, I moved in with my parents. I've made no plans to sell my home or rent it. People have said, 'You're so stupid for not selling it' and mentioned that I'm wasting money by continuing to pay the mortgage for a vacant house. They don't get that there's a mental block when it comes to my home because it's the first one I purchased with my husband. They don't understand the sentimental value or the headache of having to make repairs in order to sell it - which has to be done without his being here to guide me. I've lost so many good friends during my widowed journey. It's been really hard because each time a relationship ends, it feels like yet another loss.

Lynn, Widowed December 2015

"You don't have to defend yourself against someone's judgment. Don't feed into it. If you don't give them a response, they'll eventually stop."

CRITICISM.

FINANCES

"It's an insult to injury when you're in a fog and have to learn something as complicated as finances and planning."

The biggest lesson I've learned about finances has been that I'm capable of running my household on my own. I was lucky in that my husband and I had a pretty equal relationship and we managed our finances together. After he passed away, I realized how much I had relied on him and his input. Being alone and making decisions that affect my family is bloody scary. I had to sell our beautiful dream home we'd purchased just six months before he died. The guilt I felt was horrendous but I needed to downsize. I made a lot of money as a result yet I'm still not completely okay with it. It was a decision that needed to be made though.

Kylie, Widowed July 2015

FREEDOM.

My husband was the breadwinner and I was a stay-at-home mom. I was very fearful when it came to finances as there were no savings. His death was a huge wake-up call for me and made me realize I needed to set money aside. The main thing I would share with someone who is recently widowed is not to make any major purchases for the first six months. We go through so much that first year and it's hard to tell where you'll be financially at the end of that time.

Jennifer, Widowed July 2014

SECURITY.

I've missed paying bills due to 'widow brain'. The money was there but I simply forgot to pay it. I find I can only handle three major things at a time. I put those items on a list and as I complete the third task, I make a new list. Sometimes, I put stuff I've already done on the list just to be able to scratch it off. It's important we give ourselves credit for all we accomplish.

Susan, Widowed February 2013

PLANNING.

"I've heard I'm living off 'blood money'. My husband and I saved, invested, and had life insurance. I won't apologize for doing what we needed to do to make sure the other was taken care of if the worst happened."

"After our spouses die, we often just see a mountain of debt and try to make quick decisions. It's best to seek out a neutral third-party who can slow us down and help us get to where we need to be in the future."

I was a bit naive when it came to finances and have been taken advantage of by others who thought of me as the 'dumb single woman' or 'rich widow'. I recently had a contractor working on a few projects and thought I could trust him. I paid him a day earlier than I should have, and he promised he'd return the following day. He's not been back since. Another person owed my husband money and when I tried to collect, he told me my husband had told him the loan didn't need to be repaid. It was clearly a lie because I had my husband's phone with evidence showing otherwise. My financial advisor warned me there are two things that cause people to lose their morality: sex and money. It's helpful to have an objective person guiding me financially. He has no emotions involved and doesn't have a finger in the pie. He simply gives advice using financial knowledge.

Melinda, Widowed January 2015

I certainly don't overspend by any means but it's been difficult. I found out my husband was in debt and those financial obligations fell on to my plate. Now that there's only one income, my account has been in the negative quite a few times. I keep pushing forward though and make it a priority to 'experience' my money. Some people like to see their money by purchasing shoes and other tangible items. For me, I prefer to create memories. I'd advise widows to be cautious with their spending. Retail therapy is just a band-aid. It only makes you feel better temporarily.

Katie, Widowed January 2015

Since my husband died, money is less important to me. We used to save constantly for our future. He passed away suddenly and I realized we could have been having fun instead of setting money aside. Now, my philosophy is that if it doesn't put me into debt, I'll buy it. I take the trip versus saving money for a rainy day. I worked with a financial advisor to set up my daughter's college fund and my retirement but I still continue to live for today. We all know that tomorrow may not come.

Sharon, Widowed February 2012

GOALS.

I've had to learn to say 'no' to myself as it relates to my finances since my husband's passing. He and I typically divided the responsibilities with my taking care of paying the monthly expenses and him planning our budget and handing long-term strategic planning. I wasn't as equipped when he passed away to take over his role. In the short term, it led me down the path of some fruitless spending ('grief spending') but also took care of home improvements. With the help of my financial advisor, we developed a plan and worked together on monthly budgets. He helped me through my planning so I would not overspend and I'm very blessed to have him. It's important for widows to take a step back post-loss and not make any rash decisions such as large purchases or selling their homes. I recommend they find a financial advisor in their area who can help them navigate through all the complexities of their finances. It's a difficult journey to do on your own.

Leonor, Widowed November 2012

"I gave myself permission to be financially irresponsible in the year following my husband's death. I wasn't indulgent but if it made my children's day better, we did it."

"Avoid making major purchases for at least the first six months."

RESOURCEFUL.

"You don't have to justify your spending to anyone."

When my husband passed away, we were in terrible financial shape. The public school system in our area wasn't great; therefore, we'd sacrificed a lot to send our son to private school. Thankfully, there was life insurance to help pay off our debts. I've learned to never again live beyond my means and that material things don't matter. In talking to friends and family, I also see that based on their debt-to-income ratios, they typically don't have enough life insurance. You just never know when something will happen. My husband was in the Caribbean when he died. Thankfully, he'd purchased a $70 travel insurance policy which ended up saving me over $30,000 to get him back home. The unexpected happens more often than we think.

Kelly, Widowed August 2012

My children were 1 and 3 years old when my husband died. I'm a stay-at-home mother and felt comforted that my husband had made provisions for my children in the case of his death. It was quite a shock to find out the money he'd left couldn't be accessed until they were 16 and 18 and that doesn't help me raise them now. Even though I am their parent, I was advised that I'd have to go to court to establish guardianship and that costs nearly as much as the money they'll receive. This experience has caused me to get my own affairs in order. If I pass away, my children's caregiver will have full access to any money that I've earmarked for them. I'd encourage fellow widows to explore their options and take a look at all angles when setting up wills, trusts, and directives.

Katie, Widowed March 2016

When I was married, nothing happened financially that I didn't know about. We kept a list of each other's bank accounts, not just names but a complete, full-on list including the name of the institution, account number, log in and password in our safe. Having this information made my life much easier to do the things I needed to do— from closing accounts to dealing with the IRS. A new widow should seek out the advice of an accountant or a lawyer who is financially savvy to help her navigate current and future needs. If there isn't a life insurance policy in place or there are limited funds, she should reach out to organizations who can walk her through the legalities of widowhood free of cost. See what can be done on her own (Social Security, banking, etc.), then reach out to friends and family for recommendations. I found people were grateful to be of help and it made them feel useful. I also didn't hesitate to drop the 'widow card' as needed.

Christine, Widowed August 2012

DATING

"Follow your heart. Don't be influenced by the opinions of others. Every widow's path is uniquely her own."

It took me four years before I felt ready to open my heart to love again. It's different for every widow. Some are ready at two months, some at five months, and some never want to date. If you decide to date when you're not ready, it's going to be bad. You'll enter into many unhealthy relationships if you date for any other reason than because it's what you want. I can recall people pushing me to date but I wasn't ready. I literally threw up when the first man flirted with me post-loss. You have to listen to your gut, your heart, and your instincts. You know what's best for you.

Kelley, Widowed July 2011

"You have to know you can't replace your husband even if you find someone with the same physical characteristics."

"You'll find others will feel your decision to date is sudden. The reality is that our lost loved one isn't 'lost' from their everyday life. They don't wake up in their bed alone every morning. Time may stand still for them because the death isn't in their face."

As a stay-at-home mom, I find there are limited opportunities for organic dating like there was in my 20's and college. I have no time for the bar or to hang out. Isolation then becomes a huge part of widowhood. And, it's not self-imposed, there is just not much time to do anything. Because of my limited availability, I find I've developed a low tolerance for b.s. I can spot it a mile away. My relationships have been further apart because I have a bigger magnifying glass. From Date 1, I ask myself if the relationship is capable of going anywhere. It's all about my son. Can you fit in his life? I've met great men who didn't make it to a second or third date because my son will always come first.

Shantelle, Widowed December 2015

DISCOVERY.

"If you keep asking yourself if you're ready to date, you're probably not."

Being a widow makes you so vulnerable. It's easy to fall for whatever men tell you. That was an issue for me early on but I'm now much wiser. It's hard when you get knocked down/ rejected, but we just have to keep going. Know that it's not you; it's them. I've been dating on and off for nearly 13 years and still believe there is someone out there for me.

Cindy, Widowed January 2003

With some exception, the world is a very different place than it was well over 20 years ago when I met my husband. While my upbringing and core values are the same, I can't use the same criteria I used back then when dating now as a widow. Most men I know and like are already involved in serious relationships, and I simply will not date someone in that position. It is so different nowadays with online dating exposing us to the greatest numbers and higher chance of a good match.

I find dating is comparable to our approach to mail. There is lots of junk to sort through. Then, there is important mail (i.e. people to meet) buried in there - not necessarily with a flashy subject line - those which will have a huge, positive impact on your life. You can't throw it all out. You have to weed through that mail, trusting there are key items (people) to be found. Yes, junk mail is irritating but don't let the 'junk' break you down and try not to take it personally. Be open-minded, yet guarded. My counselor suggested I write out the core things I was looking for in a potential mate before I started dating. I was told to use them as a guideline but stay flexible and be ready to re-evaluate the list as needed. I've found this advice to be sound. That, and to simply follow your gut.

Anne-Marie, Widowed August, 2015

"If we have a foundation of self-confidence, no one will take advantage of us as we start dating."

"You're the only one who knows if you're ready to date."

We often try to replace the love we have with our spouse when dating. It goes from 'Hello' to 'You're my new boyfriend' to 'I love you'. We have to slow down and take our time getting to know potential partners. Passion and/or romance isn't a substitute for love. Just because we've been swept off our feet doesn't mean it will lead to 'happily ever after'. I looked at dating as an opportunity to meet new people. I eventually met a great guy and we got married on January 1, 2018!

Elizabeth, Widowed January 2015

FUN.

"The better care we take of ourselves, the better the people who deserve to be in our lives will treat us."

It took me two years before I was ready to start dating. My main concerns were A) Am I ready? and B) What would others say? I thought dating would enhance my grief. I had taken baby steps and I assumed it would take me right back to that depressed state. After I actually went on the first date, I realized it wasn't as scary as I'd thought. My family and friends were also very supportive of my decision. It's difficult to know when you're truly ready to start dating but you won't know until you try.

Nina, Widowed September 2014

One of the biggest lessons I've learned about dating post-loss is to not take it too seriously. It took me seven years to meet someone and while dating, I never thought of it as trying to find a new husband. It's important to relax and enjoy the ride. Widows should look out for scammers and learn how to weed them out. We often think scammers are exclusive to online dating but they can be found anywhere.

Beverly, Widowed March 2010

"For a while after my husband died, I didn't want to date. I just wanted to get laid. I ended up putting up with a man's crap because I became attached even though I swore I wouldn't. He was better than what was on the dating sites...at least I knew his crap."

"I thought I would want someone who was broken like I was...someone who would understand my loss. But, I learned a widower is no better or worse than someone who has not lost a spouse. If he's not a good person deep down, regardless of status, he will not be for me."

FRUSTRATION.

I was widowed with three children and felt I might need to settle when it came to dating. I thought any man that came along could be good enough but that was the wrong way to view dating post-loss. I now know I deserve more. I would rather be alone than to not have what I deserve. I won't go out with just anyone. My standards and expectations have changed and I'm willing to wait for the man I deserve.

Gina, Widowed September 2012

GUILT.

"Dating post-loss creates a time struggle for many widows. You want to take your time to get to know someone but you also know tomorrow isn't promised. Time wasn't as precious when we were in our 20's."

"There will be pressure from friends, family, and society but you have to be okay with being alone for a while and not rushing into dating."

The most challenging part of dating post-loss has been remembering that a new relationship doesn't have the history that comes with being married for years. We've had to have our fair share of fights and learning each other's likes and dislikes. I immediately wanted the 'team' effort that I'd had with my husband. I had to learn that you can't get to that level of a partnership without putting in the work.

Jennifer, Widowed September 2013

"How do you know when you're ready to date? Something just goes off inside of you. Suddenly, you'll start paying attention to the opposite sex, start smiling back, and eventually say, 'Wow, I think I can do this!'"

ROMANCE.

You're not the same person you were prior to losing your spouse. When it comes to dating, there's a good chance that you're not looking for the same things you needed from a relationship when you met your husband. There is no timeframe for working through a loss. People often think that because they've gotten to the one-year mark that it means they are ready to date. That's not always true. It's all about self-awareness and knowing what's best for you as an individual.

Windsor, Widowed February 2010

"We've been through enough hell. Don't be afraid to have fun... lots of it!"

SEX

"Sex is life-affirming.
There is nothing wrong
with exploring your
sexuality if you feel
comfortable and
are being safe."

There was such guilt when I began craving intimacy post-loss. It wasn't until my therapist validated my feelings that I gave myself permission to let go of much of that emotion. She said it was a good sign and that I'd simply entered a different phase of my grief. My thoughts on sex have been an evolution. I failed very miserably at my first attempt. I'd made all these arrangements and had grand plans but I ended up crying the entire night. Thankfully, I had someone who was patient and understanding. Looking back, my need at the time was more about intimacy than the physical aspect of sex. I think that's different for every widow so I cannot dictate what's appropriate or not. You have to know within yourself what you what - or don't want - from a future partner. Just be safe, regardless of the option that works best for you.

Taneshia, Widowed February 2013

"Sex can be a way for widows to find their voice again."

For me, sex and grief were intertwined. The last thing I said to my husband was 'Get off me!'. I was three months pregnant and experiencing morning sickness all day. I was not feeling well and we'd had a disagreement earlier. He tried to cuddle up with me and I pushed him away. He said, 'I love you' and went to sleep. I woke up to him dying.

Because of that experience, I wrestled with guilt and, for a long time, felt I couldn't ever turn down anyone for sex or they'd die. I jumped into a sexual relationship soon after my husband's death. Looking back, it wasn't the smartest decision I'd made but it was what I needed. I followed a pattern of jumping in and out of bed with men and I wasn't always safe about it. The men were strangers and I didn't want to have sex with people I cared about. The only person I cared for was dead. I had no control over that but I had control over my body. In my mind, I was making choices for me but grief was clouding my judgment. It wasn't until the third year that I questioned my behaviors. I don't necessarily regret my 'slutty widow phase' but it was a way to escape and pretend I wasn't really sad. I enjoyed that aspect of it but didn't like the sex. I think it's important for us to listen to those around us who have our best interest at heart when they tell us to slow down. We aren't seeing clearly when we're in the 'grief fog'.

Maheanani, Widowed September 2013

"Every widow is so different. Some use sex as a way to 'recover' while others have to wait until they've made significant steps in their healing."

When I lost my husband, I didn't know it was 'normal' for my body to crave sex. I was my harshest critic and there was lots of self-shaming. I tried to fight the urges for four months and can remember counting down the days of not having sex. It felt so unnatural but I made it to day 62. I was secretive about my sexual activity for the first two years because of religious and societal pressures... this isn't how widows behave. I then gave myself permission to do it openly and without apology; I was sick of fighting.

I often share my story as a way to let other widows know they aren't alone. I encourage everyone who has lost a spouse to find a group of like-minded people who can validate their feelings. It's important that I help remove the stigma of 'grief sex' by letting others know it is 'normal', and okay. As long as you're being safe and not indulging in sex that endangers or hurts children, you have no reason to feel ashamed.

Michelle, Widowed March 2014

There's the initial shock of your spouse's death and then there are like 5,000 secondary losses. When the doctors told me my husband was not going to make it, I can recall thinking, 'I don't get to have sex anymore?'. It wasn't something I thought about all the time but it was in the back of my mind. Missing sex certainty isn't something you bring up in bible study. I knew other widows but the lack of intimacy wasn't something I ever discussed. It wasn't until I found the Young, Widowed & Dating online support group that I was able to talk about it openly. One of the members there shared that her counselor said, 'Sex is very life-affirming'. That really stuck with me. I had had a very active sex life with my husband and then I experienced what felt like a famine. I prayed and asked God to take away my desires. I even compartmentalized it and tried to shut off that side of my brain. But, when I met my boyfriend and we kissed for the first time, it was like 'unleash the hounds!'. I gave myself permission to feel and be sexual. It was affirmation that I was still alive.

Pam, Widowed September 2014

INTIMACY.

Since the death of my husband, I have discovered myself much more. I now have a greater understanding of what I want and need. My curiosity has always been there, but now I'm learning to try new things—from porn to threesomes. Exploring yourself sexually is a beautiful thing. No matter your age or size, it's okay to get in touch with your sexuality. It might be scary at first but you have to give yourself permission to feel again.

Krystan, Widowed October 2009

"When I was first widowed, it was all about sex. Now that I'm five years in, I'm learning to respect myself again. We lose so much when our husbands die."

"We have to get over feelings that we are cheating on our late husbands. They are no longer alive so it's not cheating."

I've learned two lessons about sex post-loss. The first is that it is transactional. I had a pretty active sex life with my husband. Once he passed away, there was a carnal need to have sex. I was relentless in finding physical connections. I was hypersexual even when not acting on it. My standards were lowered and I sought out anyone who would take away the loneliness. Sex was just a transaction. I didn't even care if my needs were met, I was just satisfied that I'd had sex.

The second thing I've learned is indifference. I don't yearn to have a partner in bed with me every night but I do want someone to be at my disposal. At times I wonder if I'm a good person. While I don't go out of my way to hurt others, I think I emotionally extort people to meet my needs and I don't feel bad. It's a survival mechanism. I'm currently in an arrangement that has worked for a while. He wants more but I'm at a crossroad. I can't go through another loss. It's too raw...too much. I barely survived my husband's death and need to have something left for my children.

Carolyn, Widowed December 2012

My husband was diagnosed with cancer and we weren't intimate for the last two years of his life. It was just too painful for him. After he passed away, my libido went into overdrive. It was almost animalistic in nature. I yearned for human contact and to have a physical connection. The first time I was intimate post-loss, the guy couldn't get his clothes off fast enough. That encounter then created a monster! I eventually reigned in my 'widow slut' and was able to forgive myself for choosing to be happy and exploring my sexuality. I'd tell new widows that they are responsible for themselves and they have to live their life on their own terms. It's important to note, however, that they should only get sexually involved with someone when they are ready. They determine when that time is and it doesn't have to be based on anyone else's schedule/timeframe.

Verdeana, Widowed January 2015

"Sometimes our grief isn't reflected in a way that is helpful for us. We may be craving a connection and not necessarily sex."

Connections.

I've gone from being open with my sexuality and not having to explain date nights to now censoring that part of my life from my children. They are older and they now know how to access my phone which means constantly having to delete photos/texts. The spontaneity I enjoyed with my husband is no longer there. I have to be meticulous in scheduling time for a rendezvous. Someone joked that I have the precision of a NASA scientist!

My advice for newer widows considering a sexual relationship is to determine what it is that you want from a potential partner. If you cannot have sex without your emotions being involved, then you have to be extra careful. I've had my fun being a 'widow whore' but I'm now ready for a relationship. It's important to know the difference between those two desires.

Megan, Widowed April 2013

Lust.

"Although I know my husband would have wanted me to move forward and be happy, I still struggle at times with guilt for being intimate with another man."

"Grief sex shouldn't make you feel worse than you already do."

"Give yourself permission to embrace your sexuality."

"Sex or a new relationship doesn't eliminate grief. Maybe your partner can be part of your healing, but you really have to face your grief. It has to be acknowledged."

The fact that my husband had a heart attack during sex caused me to be fearful about future sexual encounters. The first time I was intimate post-loss was with a close friend and I warned him it may not go well. Sex is still a struggle at times but I remind myself the odds of losing another partner, in the same manner, aren't very high.

I also had to remind myself that sex isn't going to be the same - whether good or bad - because I don't have the history that I did with my husband. I was married for 20 years. We had two decades to get to know each others' bodies. No one I've met has been the same in bed as my husband. It doesn't matter how old I get or how many partners I have, everyone will be different and that's not always a negative thing.

Denise, Widowed September 2014

PERMISSION.

"It's okay to have a sexual connection with someone after the death of your spouse. Don't feel guilty."

"'Grief sex' is not a solution but if it makes you feel better, go for it!"

"Sex is an important part of living. Keep moving forward in that direction as long as it is healthy for you."

"I've found that widows are either disgusted by the thought of sex or they can't get enough of it. Neither is right or wrong."

"Some widows will be sexually active very quickly after their spouse's death, others will wait years and for some, it will never happen. All scenarios are perfectly okay."

My thoughts on sex have changed over time. I'm more confident in all aspects of my life including sex. When my husband was sick he said he hoped I'd remarry (I'm so grateful to him for that gift). The thought of being sexually active was a non-issue after his death because I was repulsed by the thought of another man touching me. Slowly, the idea of dating began to swirl in my mind. After being back in the dating world for about six months, I had sex. I had been very happy with my husband and never questioned our sex life. With this man; however, I found I was open to trying new things and being more adventurous. Since I can't have my life with my husband, the life I wanted, it made me question what I want to have now. I'm more willing to be open to new experiences. It's important for us as widows to pursue whatever makes us feel good while protecting our hearts.

Caroline, Widowed May 2012

"Sex is completely normal and it's okay to have a high libido post-loss. It's a natural response to trauma."

DESIRES.

RELIGION & SPIRITUALITY

"You have to believe that your spiritual path will take you exactly where you need to be."

My faith has gone the entire spectrum since the death of my husband. There is no doubt that the death of a spouse tests your faith. I was angry at God and angry at my husband. I was also conflicted because I didn't know my purpose. A Catholic priest told me not to be angry at my spouse. He said, 'Be angry at God because He can handle it'. Now, I have a much deeper understanding of God's plan in my life. I'm very involved in the American Cancer Society in honor of my husband and I can talk to others about my journey. I would never have gotten to this place of comfort and peace if I hadn't lived this life. My faith allows me to trust where God is now leading me.

Tina, Widowed June 2001

"Christians are often rushed to 'get over' a loss. If we don't 'heal' quickly then we're accused of being weak in our faith or that there is a lack of trust in God."

I've always believed in God. When my husband was in the hospital, we kept praying. My son asked for a sign that his dad would get better but he eventually passed away. He felt God had let him down. My daughter handled her grief by becoming agnostic. I continued to pray for them. About three years ago, my son asked if we could go into a church and he's been regularly attending service ever since. I've clung to my faith even more now that I'm widowed - not just for me but also for my kids. I know what I hold in my heart will protect them as well.

Loyda, Widowed April 2009

PEACE.

"Losing a spouse is so different when your faith is strong in Jesus. It really changes your perspective on how you grieve."

My religion has always been a constant in my life, but I definitely questioned my spirituality when my husband died. I wouldn't say I walked away from it because I knew it was okay to be angry and ask questions. During the first six months of my grief, I attended church without being present in the moment and at times didn't even want to be there. God, however, waited patiently until I was ready to re-establish our relationship. He was there for me when I wasn't there for Him.

Sarah, Widowed October 2014

My husband's death caused me to question some aspects of my faith. I am Jewish and had a very religious upbringing. My husband's family wasn't as religious so I was responsible for the religious aspects of our household. A year before my husband died, he met a Rabbi and started embracing our faith more. Both our families became especially close. When my husband died, I assumed the Rabbi would help guide me through the ceremonial seven-day mourning period. I quickly learned I was excluded from certain aspects of the ceremony simply because I am a woman.

I question my own religion doing this to me at the worst possible time in my life. It was the beginning of my anger and honestly, I haven't completely gotten over it. I find it challenging to marry my religion and spirituality with the fact that women in some aspects of my faith are considered secondary in religious ceremonies. I recently met a great group of people with whom I more closely identify spiritually so I'm moving forward and working on letting go of my anger.

Lisa, Widowed September 2014

DIVINITY.

Two months before my husband's cancer diagnosis, as I was taking down Christmas decorations, I heard a voice ask, 'What are you going to do next year when he's not here?'. I've always been a believer in Christ and feel that was His way of helping me prepare for my husband's death. From diagnosis to death was four months. I am so blessed and so grateful that the Holy Spirit allowed us the opportunity to say all the things we wanted to say to each other. The circumstances surrounding my husband's illness and death have made me spiritually stronger. I've learned that if I try to do things on my own, it doesn't work out. I have to put it in the hands of a higher power.

Janet, Widowed June 2013

"After my husband died, I saw God as being bigger than my denomination allowed Him to be. This revelation was very freeing. I was no longer bound by the traditional and legalistic rules of that religion."

"Christians often say God doesn't give us more than we can bear. That's just not true. In 2nd Corinthians 1:8, Paul talks about being shipwrecked and says 'We were under great pressure, far beyond our ability to endure, so that we despaired even of life'. What the Bible does say is that we will not be tempted beyond what we can bear. Feeling despair from circumstances and being tempted are different."

COMFORT.

FAITH.

It's rarely talked about in widowed circles but it's a struggle trying to be faithful to your religion when you lose a spouse. While we're married, it's spiritually 'legal' to have sex. An active, healthy lifestyle is even encouraged. But for the widow who is married on Thursday but widowed on Friday, what does that mean for her sex life? Yes, the mind and spirit know that sex should be reserved for marriage, but the body doesn't understand.

Many Christian widows have a deep desire to wait for God's timing. In the first year, we're not necessarily thinking about sex because we're in a fog. In the second year, we feel full of energy and determined to stay the course with our faith and beliefs. What happens when Year 2 turns to Year 7 and there is no husband in sight though? I'm not a eunuch, monk, or nun - it gets hard as time goes on. I know the Bible encourages us to have self-control and I've been doing that for years. It's just impossible to turn off that urge. I have had many talks with God about being forced into celibacy and how it feels like I'm being punished unfairly.

LaTisha, Widowed March 2011

"It's okay to grieve even as a Christian. You are a human going through a very human process. To grieve is to be human."

"We have to learn to pray and praise Him in the midst of suffering."

"Grief is biblical and we're supposed to process it. The Bible points out that mourning is limited, yet there is no timeframe for grief."

Even though my husband was agnostic, his guidance - since his death - has reinforced my spirituality. Two minutes after his passing, I said, 'I miss you already' and felt him say, 'I'm right here'. It was so clear that I looked around to see if my mother-in-law had felt his presence too. He was an engineer and I continue to receive signs from him such as sequential, repeating numbers on everything from clocks to license plates. His death has taught me to trust my intuition, which is closely tied to my spirituality. I'm learning to pay attention to it more.

Katherine, Widowed July 2014

My husband's death has taught me that everything happens for a reason. I know that's very controversial in the world of widowhood but I've found it to be true. Not long after my father passed away, I was invited to a meeting where a client was launching a new greeting card line for grandparents. It was especially difficult for me and a coworker hugged me and explained that she too had lost her dad. She said she didn't question why that awful thing had happened to her because she knew she was stronger than her friends and could handle the loss of a parent. In losing her dad and being strong, she was able to be a resource for friends who would eventually experience a parent's death.

At my husband's funeral, I vividly recall looking out and seeing our friends and family and remembering the conversation I'd had with that coworker. It was true: none of my friends could have handled the loss of their spouses at such a young age. Though it's been a very difficult journey, I am comforted knowing that I'm able to be there for others.

Jacqueline, Widowed January 2012

The main thing I've learned about my faith post-loss has been God's sovereignty and understanding that He has plans that trump what I want. There is a God. He is the God of the Bible. He is good. But I am not Him. The Bible verse Isaiah 55: 8-9 becomes very much true when you've experienced the loss of a spouse.

My faith has always been strong but when you pray for healing and your husband isn't healed the way you'd like, it's difficult. I've wrestled with the Lord and come to know Him in a better and deeper way. We're often told not to question God but even Job complained and wrestled with Him. Job 42:5 says 'My ears had heard of you, but now my eyes have seen you' and that has also been true in my own life since my loss. I'm a therapist and God has shown me my husband's death wasn't in vain. I am much more compassionate on both a professional and personal level. I believe God uses our suffering to allow us to minister to others and this brings purpose and meaning to my loss. 2 Corinthians 1:4 and Romans 8:28-29 have become true in my own life. As a Christian widow, my grief isn't the same as a nonbeliever. I'm able to grieve with hope. My husband was a strong believer in Christ and I know I'll be reunited with him in heaven. Death is temporary. It's real and it hurts but I'm comforted knowing I'll be with him again.

Ann, Widowed March 2013

I am much more focused on my spirituality and less on adhering to a formal religious practice post-loss. I used to seek comfort in the structure of attending Mass for example, and now I get more comfort out of contemplating my purpose and my spirit's journey. I have also become open to the possibility of reincarnation, which prior to losing my husband I hadn't given much thought to. Although my new views on spirituality post-loss are so different from what I was raised to believe, it doesn't mean I am not still religious… it just means that my suffering has brought me a new level of perspective. I think it is important for anyone living with a loss to keep searching for how to give meaning to their suffering. Find a way to have it help you leave this life better than it was when you entered it.

Anna, Widowed February 2015

"We must choose to praise God for who He is. He doesn't change because of our loss. He is worthy of praise regardless of what we've been through."

REBUILDING

"Initially, it's hard to envision that you'll ever be happy again or that better days are ahead. You have to keep hoping, if not for you, do it for your children and family."

Prior to my husband's passing, my whole life was focused on my marriage and my children. I got married at 19 years old so the titles of 'wife' and 'mom' came quickly. Looking back, I'm not sure I had an opportunity to know myself. Since I've been widowed, I've learned that in order to get myself out of the black hole of grief, I needed to do something each day that would bring me a smile or help me get out of bed. Each day, that 'thing' got bigger. I soon discovered my needs and realized I shouldn't feel guilty for having them.

I encourage new widows, who can't imagine happiness on the other side of loss, to focus on breathing. Start with five minutes then build up to an hour and then half a day. If that's all you're able to focus on, that's okay. Some days, it'll be all you're responsible for doing.

Stacey, Widowed December 2011

"When you lose a spouse, you find an amazing strength you never knew you had."

GRACE.

I'm learning to be patient with the rebuilding stage of widowhood. Death changes you and you have to learn who you are after a loss. For me, this involves prayer and my faith. I started with daily devotions, learning how to trust God. I knew He had a plan and it was based on His timing, not mine. A widow friend told me God has to prepare my heart for what's in store and I believe that. My husband's death has drawn me closer to my faith.

There are some days when I take two steps forward and others when all I can do is breathe. My advice for myself is the same as I'd tell another widow: If you can't see beyond today, just focus on getting through the next minute.

Libby, Widowed August 2014

"I was born again the day my husband died. I'm not the same person I was once was."

The biggest lesson I've learned about life after loss is how to trust my own decisions. During my marriage, I got accustomed to running my decisions by my husband. Now that he's not here, I've had to do things on my own. As time has gone on, I've gotten better at trusting myself which has given me more confidence.

If I'm being completely honest - and, I know this is hard to digest - I've built a better life post-loss than the one I had before. Don't get me wrong, I had a great marriage. But, instead of the 19/20-year-old girl that I was, I got to start over as an experienced woman and I decided how I wanted to rebuild my life. It's been very rewarding.

It's important to realize that rebuilding our lives is a process. It's never complete. For example, we may add a new partner and find there are challenges getting back to the 'give and take' of a relationship. I'd encourage newer widows to seek out a support group. Hearing 'me too' is an important part of the healing and rebuilding process.

Keri, Widowed September 2015

"I don't want to merely survive. There is a lot of life left in me and I want to live it."

"It's hard to figure out who I am post-loss. I'm re-learning myself and friends and family are learning this new person I've become."

Kerry Phillips

REBIRTH.

When my husband died, I honestly didn't know if I could make it on my own. I've always had his support. But, I did it! I bought a house, went back to school, and accomplished other things I never imagined doing alone. Even though friends assured me it would get better, I didn't believe them because I was so distraught at the time. It turns out they were right; there is light at the end of the tunnel. Last summer I was given a free surfing lesson and, as I was out in the water, it hit me: I was happy. I'd pushed through my husband's illness, my breast cancer diagnosis, his death, and the bilateral mastectomy to reclaim my life. I finally feel back to my self.

As much as it hurts, it's important for widows to know that it will be okay. Be sure to reach out when you need support and accept help and resources from others as well.

Alicia, Widowed September 2014

"I am such a different person now. Although I miss my husband, I don't ever want to return to the person I was before he died."

"I was sitting on a couch, smoking a cigarette and another widow posted on social media that if we fail to make the best of our lives, a year later we'd be in the same spot. That was truly my wake-up call. I'd been reduced to a minimal existence. My son was watching me. I wanted more for me, more for my son. I had to engage in life again. I've since opened a private practice offering psychotherapy with an emphasis on grief."

"Just because you're widowed doesn't mean life stops. It's just the opposite. It's where life can begin."

"Sometimes you have to go through some mess to learn empathy."

In rebuilding my life, I've learned to live in the moment. I used to worry about everything and spent 12-14 hours a day running my home daycare. When my husband died, I realized I could no longer live the way I had been. I sold my house and business and I'm so much happier. I'm doing things my way and don't care what people think. The worst thing has already happened. I survived and am moving forward with my life. In reinventing myself, I found my voice.

My husband loved life. My gift to him is enjoying this present I've been given. It's a dishonor to him to not live my best life. Even though I fail at times, I just take breaths and ask myself, 'Will this matter next week?'.

I want the next wave of widows to know they are going to be okay. Focus on the right now - that's all you have to do. Learn how to deal with your anxiety and triggers when they hit. Figure out how to ground yourself and breathe through it. Also, know your husband's energy is still with you, regardless of your belief.

Stephanie, Widowed September 2015

"For so long, my marriage was about getting my husband clean. I'd forgotten how to love. Re-learning love has been part of my rebuilding post-loss."

"What would your spouse want for you? Would he want you to stop living your life and mourn every day?"

The most important lesson of my rebuilding has been transparency. My husband died of an overdose and, for so long, I felt ashamed. I felt judged by widows who had lost their spouse to an illness and found others treated me as though there was an issue with me because of his manner of death. I went into a deep depression.

I eventually realized there were people across the country who shared my experiences and struggles. I didn't have to hide anymore. Drug-related deaths affect people of all walks of life - regardless of age, race and income.

I founded an online support group, Losing a Spouse or Loved One from Drug/Alcohol Addiction, and connected with so many who had the same challenges. It's helped tremendously with my healing. In being open and honest, I took charge of my health, losing 70 pounds. This is the best I've felt. I also never thought love would find me again, but it has. I want every widow who is in the thick of her grief to know that there is light on the other side.

CHOICE.

Renae, Widowed January 2012

After my husband died, I discovered he was leading a double life. As part of my healing and rebuilding, I had to learn to leave the past in the past. I had to focus on the good times and keep looking forward. I gave myself daily reminders to stay positive including this quote which I saved on a white board and used as a screen saver on both my phone and computer:

'One day, everything will make perfect sense. So for now, laugh at the confusion, smile through the tears and keep reminding yourself that everything happens for a reason.'

I know most widows hate hearing 'everything happens for a reason' but I've moved through the pain of his loss and can now look at it as a blessing. If he had not passed away, I would not have had my youngest son, I would not be a college graduate, and I would not be the person I am today.

Another lesson I've learned along my journey is that others' opinions of you aren't your business. Don't worry about making others happy; live your life for you.

Chrissy, Widowed March 2013

I've learned life goes on whether you want it to or not. There were days when I wanted to die too but I had to move forward for my children. Even now, some days are still hard. I believe I'm happy again though I wonder if I truly am. Though I'm not 100 percent sure, I do know that I try really hard to happy.

My sister, who lost a son, gave me great advice when she said, 'There's going to come a time when you can think of the person you lost and not cry'. I believe that. It may not be tomorrow or even five years from now but in the end, it'll be okay.

Annmarie, Widowed June 2015

"After a tragedy, every force imaginable will come against us to cause us to lose whatever hope we have left to rebuild. But, we have to keep fighting. Sometimes life isn't fair, and sometimes it appears that we have to fight twice as hard just to even the playing field. But, never-the-less, we have to keep pushing to rebuild as our stories of redemption continue to evolve."

LIVE.

A large part of rebuilding one's life post-loss is making the decision to do so. There are two moments in my life that helped shaped the person I would eventually become following the death of my husband. I remember being frustrated and telling him that his last day on Earth would be my second to last one. He replied, 'That's the stupidest thing I've ever heard. Your job if I don't make it is to win at life. If you want to remarry, do it. If you want to adopt a baby, go for it.'.

The second incident occurred after his death. I was sitting in a fetal position in the corner of the little room at the hospital where they put you after your husband dies in the ER. It was there that I decided I was going to kick ass at life. If I hadn't made that commitment to myself, I would have fallen apart completely. I was very unhealthy and overweight. Now, I am doing things I never thought I could - weightlifting competitions, career and life coaching, and public speaking, and am so much less afraid to fail at things than ever before. If I were told eight years ago that I'd be where I am now, I would never have believed it.

Sometimes, the best thing we can do as widows is to sit with our grief and acknowledge it. Don't try to self-medicate or out-exercise it. It's okay that today sucks. Allow yourself to feel it.

Diana, Widowed October 2009

I've learned the tunnel to get to the other side of grief is a lot longer and darker than I initially thought. There have been unexpected hurdles and potholes that impeded the progress I thought I should have been making.

Part of rebuilding is being able to see things from a different perspective. It's not the destination, but the journey. I told my therapist I needed a word for this place I now am in life. To have a label placed on it is to give me power over it. She called it my 'chrysalis'. I'm getting ready to change but just as the butterfly doesn't know it's becoming a butterfly, I'm not sure of the person I'm becoming.

This is where I have to trust that I'll come out on the other side and be okay. As my therapist said, 'What 10-year-old says I can't wait to plan my husband's funeral one day?' Widowhood definitely wasn't on my roadmap of life. This year; however, I'm coming out of the shock and assessing who I am. I'm learning what's at my core and discovering who I was before I was a wife and a mother.

My advice for newer widows is to get back to the bare necessities. Maybe you don't shower today. Sleep when your children sleep. Take in the small things that can propel you to the next day. It's all about self-care and loving yourself especially when you think no one else does.

Angela, Widowed July 2014

EVOLVE.

ABOUT KERRY PHILLIPS

Kerry was widowed in 2012 at age 32 when her husband was misdiagnosed while overseas. Determined to not allow grief to drag her under or for death to get a 'bonus' spouse, she vowed to successfully navigate widowhood, despite not knowing any peers who had lost a spouse.

In 2015, she realized there wasn't a forum for widows and widowers wanting to venture back into the world of dating and started Young, Widowed & Dating. The online support group provides a safe, supportive and nonjudgmental environment for the widowed community to share their dating adventures—hits and misses.

Her weekly blog of the same name covers topics ranging from relationships with in-laws to dating while raising children and everything in between. Kerry is also a blogger for Hope for Widows Foundation, a nonprofit organization which provides peer to peer support, and a former contributor to HuffPost, where she covered topics such as widowhood, loss, and grieving.

She continues to advocate for the widowed community as well as educate non-widows about the nuances of loss and grief. She is the author of "Writing & Widowing: Journaling the Journey", journal prompts designed specifically for those who have lost a spouse, and is featured in the book, "Widowed but not Wounded: The Hustle & Flow of 13 Resilient Black Widowed Women" which was released in December 2017.

You can learn more about Kerry Phillips by visiting www.YoungWidowedandDating.com.

ACKNOWLEDGMENTS

A huge debt of gratitude to the 100 widows who volunteered to be part of this project - even when you weren't exactly sure of my plans.

I thank each of you for your trust and honesty and being vulnerable with me as you shared your stories of struggles, hope, and rebuilding.

For the widows who went searching high and low for photos to include in this project, I am forever grateful. I know it must have been difficult reliving each of those memories. Thank you!

There is an Iyanla Vanzant quote that says, 'When you stand and share your story in an empowering way, your story will heal you and your story will heal someone else'. It is my wish that in reflecting and sharing your "ONE THING", you were able to heal - even a little - and find comfort in the fact that your words may ultimately impact another widow's story.

Love and light to my #WidowedPosse!

PHOTO CREDITS

Images appear courtesy of the widow pictured.

The following photographers are also acknowledged for their amazing work and allowing their image(s) to be included in the book:

Page 16 - Libby McGowan Photography

Page 17 and 21 (bottom) - Kristen Anne Photography

Page 19 and 72- Muse Photography

Page 23 - Jan Ivar Vik Photography

Page 24 (left) and 193 - Inta G Photography

Page 28 (top left) - Placek Photography & Design

Page 31, 32, 35 (left) and 36 - Becky Petty Photography

Page 33 - Aimee Crandall Photography

Page 38 - Elna Woods Photography

Page 50 (top right) - Jocelin Thure Photography

Page 57 - Smith Photography

Kerry Phillips

Page 63 (left) - Tasha Prescott Photography

Page 63 (top right) - Larissa Photography

Page 67 - Omoir Photography

Page 68 (bottom right) - Ceraolo Photography

Page 69, 76 (left), 96, 107, 112, 134, 161, 164, 167 and 179 - Stocksnap Photography

Page 73- Dov Israeli Photography

Page 76 (right) and 170 - Mojica Photography

Page 78 - J. Urban Photography

Page 87 - Stockpic Photography

Page 91 - Scott Webb Photography

Page 95 (left) - Kim Lancaster-Brantley Photography

Page 98 (top left) - D&L Photograpy

Page 98 (bottom right) - David Marino Photography

Page 106 - Michael Lund Photography

Page 108 - Myriams Fotos

Kerry Phillips